Fantastic Monsters

Contents

Written by Hawys Morgan

Illustrated by Vlad Stankovic

Collins

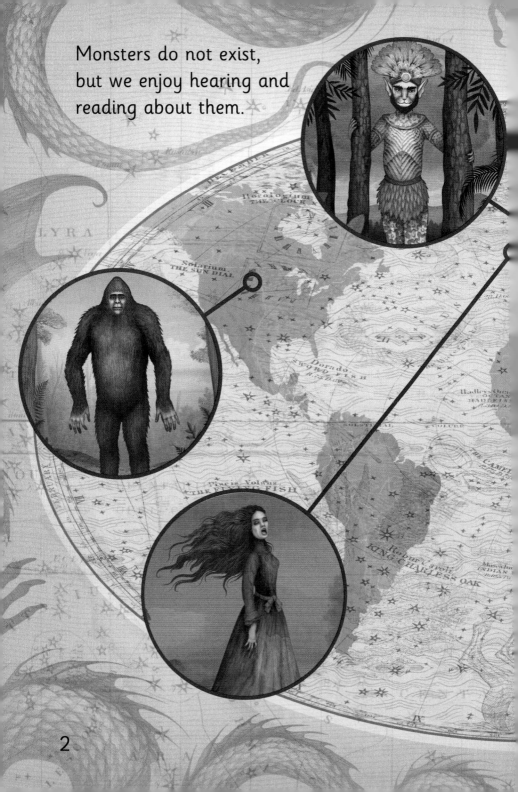

Monsters do not exist,
but we enjoy hearing and
reading about them.

2

We enjoy seeing them in art, statues, books and films.

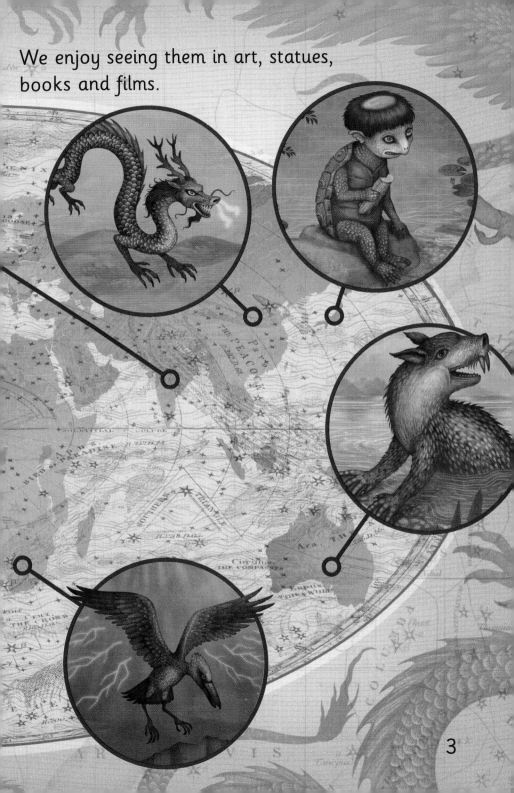

A **banshee** is a spirit that wails and screams.

4

The sound of the banshee means bad luck for the human that hears it.

5

Big foot inhabit mountains. They smell foul and can destroy trees.

Bunyips inhabit rivers and streams. They have a loud bark!

round skull

mouth

A western **dragon** has wings.
Clouds come from its nostrils.

An eastern dragon looks similar, but without wings. It can turn itself into a stream or river.

Some say an **elf** will clean, mend and cook feasts for humans!

Medusa was a Greek **gorgon**. If you looked at Medusa's swaying serpent hair, you turned into a statue!

Griffins are part bird. They represent strength.

wings

beak

At night, **imps** sneak about, steal food and play tricks.

Jinn dwell in trees, woods, underground and in the air. They cannot be seen by humans.

Kappa are found in streams.
They love cucumbers and are clever.

J
K

The **lightning bird** is as big as a human.

L

As it flies, it summons thunder and lightning. Its eggs can heal human diseases.

L

Mermaids and **mermen** lie gleaming on beaches.

M
N
O
P
Q

They swim and play in blue seas and bays.
They enjoy music and singing.

Beneath the sea, **sea serpents** lurk.
They destroy ships.

They leap out of the sea and squirt spray into the air.

snout

Unicorn means one horn.

22

If you are unwell, drink from a unicorn horn and you will be healed.

A **warg** is a hound that has sharp teeth in its big mouth.

They leap from rocks and howl at
the gleaming moon.

Medusa – Queen of the Gorgons

As a girl, Medusa was not a gorgon. A mean Greek goddess turned her into one.

There were three gorgons. Medusa was the queen.

Monsters around us

a unicorn on a coin

a mermaid painting

a dragon lantern

a griffin coat of arms

a gorgon statue

a red dragon on the Welsh flag

Fantastic monsters dwell here!

air

mountains

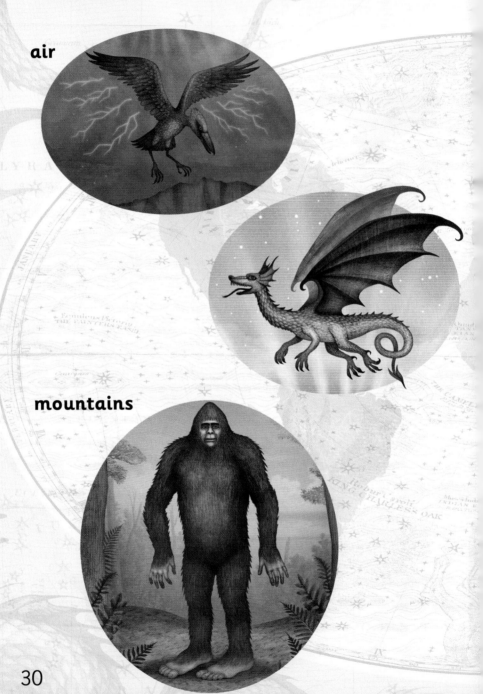